Astronomers Through Time

Lisa E. Greathouse

Earth and Space Science Readers: Astronomers Through Time

Publishing Credits

Editorial Director
Dona Herweck Rice

Associate Editor
Joshua BishopRoby

Editor-in-Chief
Sharon Coan, M.S.Ed.

Creative Director
Lee Aucoin

Illustration Manager
Timothy J. Bradley

Publisher
Rachelle Cracchiolo, M.S.Ed.

Science Contributor
Sally Ride Science

Science Consultants
William B Rice,
Engineering Geologist
Nancy McKeown,
Planetary Geologist

Teacher Created Materials
5301 Oceanus Drive
Huntington Beach, CA 92649-1030
http://www.tcmpub.com

ISBN 978-0-7439-0562-6

Printed by: VIN#973
Printed In: China
P011140

Table of Contents

Did You Know?

Ancient cultures thought that the sight of a comet, eclipse, or a new star was a sign that the gods were angry. They thought it meant war, disease, or even death was heading their way!

Astronomers: Looking Up, Looking Forward

Since the beginning of time, humans have looked to the heavens with wonder. The study of the universe is called astronomy. Ancient astronomers looked at movements in the sun, moon, and stars to help guide travelers. They also used them to keep track of the days and seasons.

In this book, you will read about some astronomers who have made a big impact in this field. They have changed what we know about the universe and our place in it. Some even risked their lives by saying that Earth was not the center of the universe. You'll learn why. Most of them never dreamed that one day humans would walk on the moon or launch a spacecraft to Pluto!

The great thing about astronomy is that there is still so much left to learn. Today's astronomers still make discoveries all the time!

Hypatia of Alexandria

Astronomy is an ancient science. Hypatia of Alexandria is a woman of ancient times. She was an expert in math. She was also an inventor and a philosopher. But she is mainly remembered as the first woman **astronomer**.

Her father raised her alone. He was the director of the university in Alexandria. He taught his daughter everything he knew. She was a very good student.

Hypatia did not marry. She chose instead to focus on her studies. During her life, she designed many tools for astronomy. She also wrote books about astronomy and edited her father's books, too.

This drawing shows what Hypatia might have looked like.

The moon's Crater Hypatia and Rima Hypatia are name in honor of Hypat

Hypatia had many students who followed her teachings. She was admired by many. But she also had enemies. She often spoke of religion and science. Not everyone in the city followed the same religion. Many were Christians. Hypatia was a pagan. Some Christians disagreed with what Hypatia had to say. They said that since she didn't follow their religion, all her work was worthless.

One day while she was riding, she was pulled from her carriage. A mob took her to a church. There, they beat and tortured her. Finally, they killed her. They burned her remains in the town center as a warning to others.

This engraving shows Hypatia being attacked by an angry mob.

So, You Want to Become an Astronomer?

If you are interested in a career in astronomy, take as many math and science classes as you can. You can also join a beginners' astronomer society. There you can learn how to use a telescope. You can meet others with an interest in space. An astronomer also needs good writing and computer skills. In college, you would need to major in astronomy or physics. Then you would need to go to graduate school.

Another interesting career is astrobiology. That is the study of life beyond Earth. You would study different planets and moons to see if life could exist on them. You would need to be an expert in both astronomy and biology. Biology is the study of living things.

Nicholas Copernicus (1473-1543)

Five hundred years ago, people believed that Earth was the center of the **solar system**. They thought that the sun, moon, stars, and other planets revolved around it. That was until Nicholas Copernicus came along. Copernicus was born in Poland in 1473. He studied law and medicine in Italy, and astronomy in Poland. Astronomy was something he especially enjoyed, like a hobby.

Copernicus figured out that the sun is at the center of the solar system.

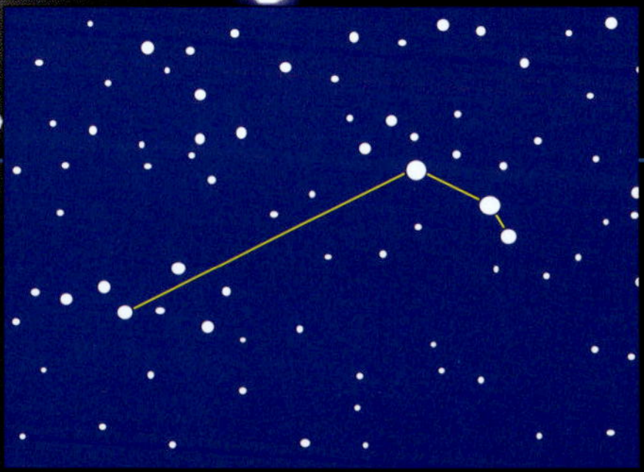

Aries

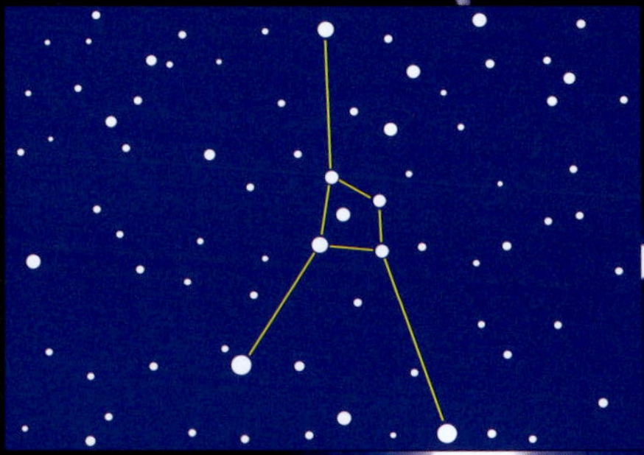

Cancer

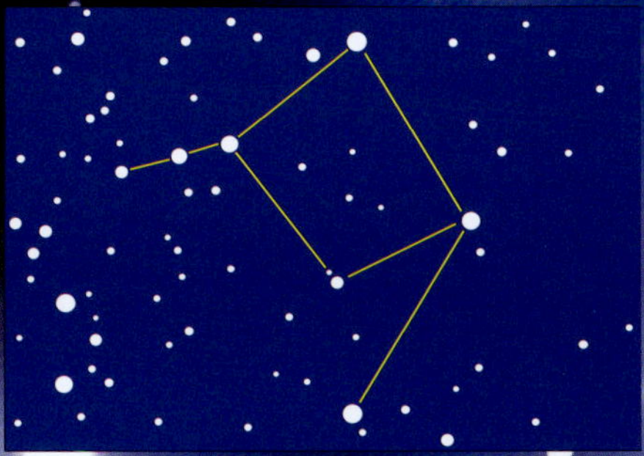

Libra

Constellations

Constellations are formations of stars. From ancient times, people have looked into the night sky at stars. They imagined the stars made shapes of things they knew. For example, in these stars they saw a ram (Aries), a crab (Cancer), and a balance (Libra).

Some people believed the constellations had special powers. Today, people who study the power of the stars and planets are called astrologers. Some people confuse astrology with astronomy. But they are not the same things at all.

Look into the sky on some star-filled night. What do you see?

Copernicus was one of the first scientists to argue that the sun is at the center of the solar system. He also said that Earth spins once a day as it orbits the sun. Most people didn't believe him. Later, the books Copernicus wrote helped other astronomers figure out how the universe works.

Copernicus died in 1543. He didn't know that one day he would be called the founder of modern astronomy.

Galileo Galilei (1564-1642)

Galileo Galilei was one of history's greatest scientists. He was born in Italy. He was the son of a famous musician. His father wanted him to be a doctor. Galileo was more interested in math. He never got a degree, but he still became a math professor and an inventor. He invented an early calculator to help solve math problems. In 1609, he heard that something called a spy glass had been invented. It was a tool that made distant objects appear closer. Galileo built one himself. He called it a **telescope**.

Galileo's telescope

the Milky Way

moon craters

modern telescope

Galileo's telescope wasn't very powerful. He still made many discoveries when he pointed it at the night sky. He saw craters on the moon. He saw stars in the Milky Way. He studied sunspots on the sun. He spotted four bodies orbiting Jupiter. He wrote of his discoveries in Italian instead of Latin. That made it easier for most people to read about them. Galileo was named court mathematician in Florence, Italy. That gave him more time to study.

The more Galileo studied, the more he became convinced that Copernicus was right. He wrote books that said the sun was the center of the solar system. Most people still believed that Earth was the center of the universe. They thought the sun and planets revolved around the Earth. The Catholic Church believed this, too. The church put Galileo on trial.

The church accused Galileo of being a **heretic**. That was a person who didn't agree with the church's teachings. Some people were put to death for this crime. In 1633, Galileo was ordered to spend the rest of his life in prison. He also was told that he could no longer say that Earth moved around the sun. Because he was ill, Galileo was allowed to serve his sentence at home. He died in 1642 at his home in Florence.

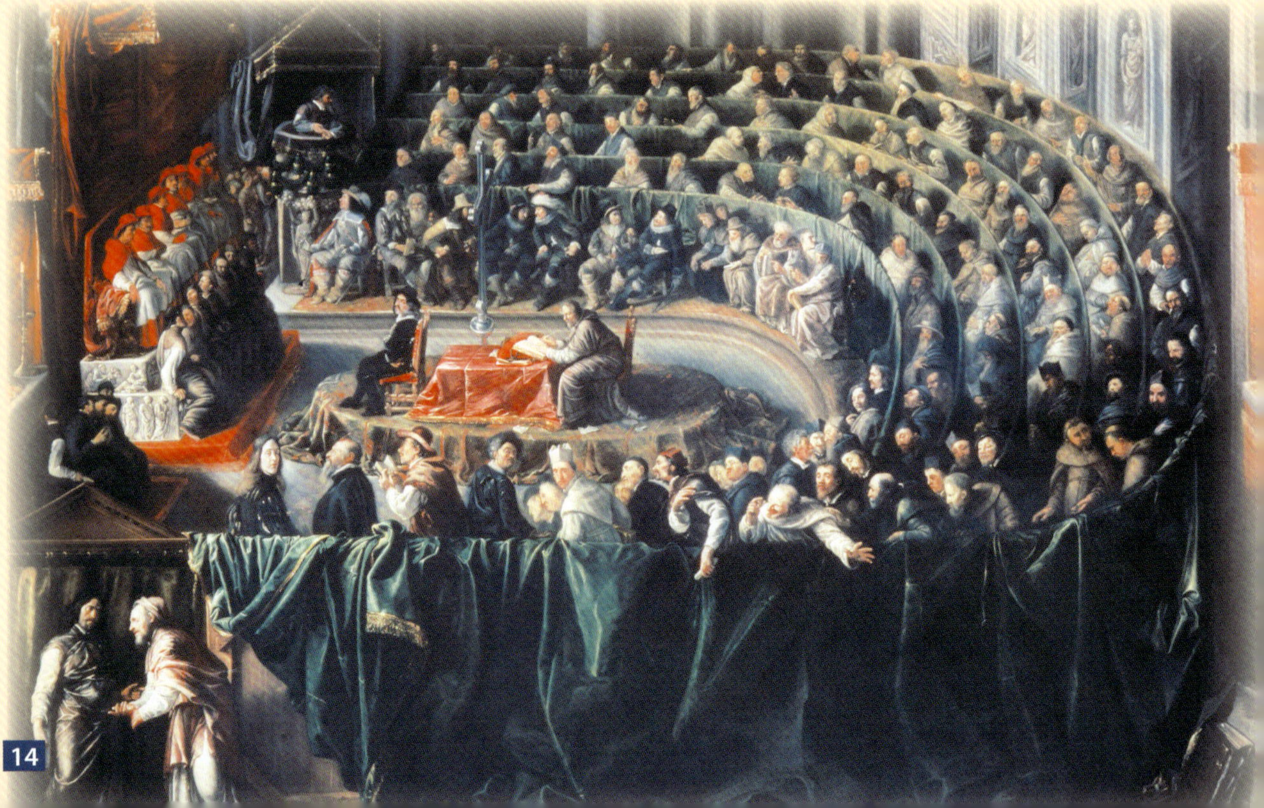

Galileo Lives On

In 1989, an unmanned spacecraft named after Galileo was launched to explore Jupiter.

It wasn't until 1992 that the church admitted that it was wrong and Galileo was right. The Earth does revolve around the sun. All those years later, Galileo was finally cleared of the charges against him!

Galileo on trial by the church

Sir Isaac Newton (1642-1727)

Isaac Newton is considered one of the greatest scientists who ever lived. His work had a big effect on astronomy, physics, math, and more.

Newton had a hard childhood. He was born in England just after his father died. He went to live with his grandparents when he was only three. Newton came from a family of farmers. His mother wanted him to become a farmer, too. But he was always studying and dreaming. Finally, his mother gave in. Newton made it to college. He had to work as a servant to pay his way through school.

copy of Newton's reflecting telescope

Newton had planned to study law. He became interested in philosophy and math. Many of his best ideas came after he earned his degree and returned home. In less than two years, he made major advances in math, physics, optics, and astronomy. Later, Newton became a math professor. His studies led to his invention of the reflecting telescope. It's the basic design for all large telescopes used today. He also came up with the branch of mathematics known as calculus.

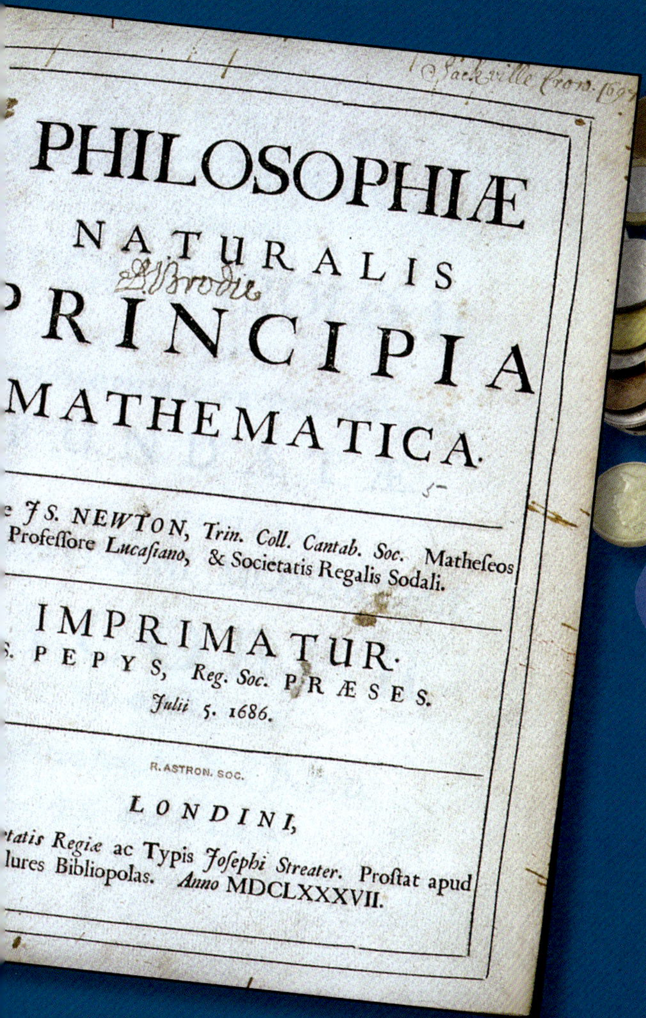

PHILOSOPHIÆ
NATURALIS
PRINCIPIA
MATHEMATICA.

JS. NEWTON, Trin. Coll. Cantab. Soc. Matheseos
Professore Lucasiano, & Societatis Regalis Sodali.

IMPRIMATUR.
S. PEPYS, Reg. Soc. PRÆSES.
Julii 5. 1686.

R. ASTRON. SOC.

LONDINI,
tatis Regiæ ac Typis Josephi Streater. Prostat apud
lures Bibliopolas. Anno MDCLXXXVII.

Did You Know?

In his later years, Newton became interested in money. He became Master of the Royal Mint in 1699. He developed ways to prevent counterfeiting of English money.

Legend has it that seeing an apple fall gave Newton his most famous idea. It had to do with **gravity**. Newton thought that gravity not only makes an apple fall to the ground. It also rules the motions of planets and stars.

From this idea, Newton discovered the law of gravity. He also came up with his famous three laws of motion. He published books about his work. This made Newton a leader in scientific research all over the world.

Newton's Laws

Newton may be most famous for his three laws of motion. They explain why things move and why they stop moving. The first law says that something that is moving will keep moving at the same speed and in the same way unless something else stops or changes it. The second law says that something will move in the same direction as the force acting on it. The third law says that for every action made, there is an equal and opposite reaction.

Caroline Herschel

Caroline Lucretia Herschel, called Lina, was born in Germany in 1759. Diseases left her face scarred, her left eye misshapen, and her body very short. Her mother said she was only fit to be a maid. Her father didn't agree. He taught her what he knew. It was her brother who really made a difference. He taught her music and helped her learn to sing. She became a skilled opera singer. Then, when he began to study astronomy, she became his assistant. Although she was never trained in math, she did all of the challenging calculations for his work. When he was away, she explored astronomy on her own. In 1786, she used a telescope to discover a comet. It became known as the "first lady's comet."

Carl Sagan (1934-1996)

Carl Sagan is sometimes called "the astronomer of the people." That's because he made astronomy popular with the public. Many people today know about astronomy because of his work. He loved astronomy so much that he made many other people love it, too. Many astronomers today say that Sagan's work first made them interested in space.

Sagan was born in New York. Even as a young boy, he read about space all the time. He earned three different science degrees. Then he became a professor himself.

Sagan wrote over two dozen books about space. He won a Pulitzer Prize. That's a famous award for writing. His TV series *Cosmos* was one of the most-watched shows in television history. Sagan even helped NASA with U.S. space missions to Venus, Mars, and Jupiter.

Sagan helped NASA design and build a robot that was sent to Mars.

Carl Sagan with the *Viking* Mars lander.

A famous movie called *Contact* is based on one of Sagan's books. It is all about people coming into contact with life on other planets. Many science stories that came before gave the idea that aliens would be harmful to humans. Sagan thought aliens would be friendly and helpful.

Sagan was one of the first scientists to suggest that there might be life on other planets. He was convinced of it. In fact, he thought it was silly to think otherwise. With all the stars, planets, and galaxies in the universe, he was sure that some of them would hold life. He urged NASA to explore the solar system for signs of life.

Jodie Foster in the movie *Contact*

Is Anyone Out There?

In 1972, Sagan and his wife wrote a message in pictures to aliens. The messages were attached to the *Pioneer* space probes. These unmanned spaceships escaped the solar system and entered outer space. The Sagans hoped there were beings in space who would read their messages one day.

Henrietta Swan Leavitt

Henrietta Swan Leavitt was born in 1868. Although many women did not attend college during her time, she did. After graduating, she became ill. Her illness left her nearly deaf. That didn't stop her. She became a research assistant at a college **observatory**. Observatories are places where people look at and study objects in space. At first she was a volunteer there. Seven years later, she was hired for 30 cents an hour.

While there, she noticed that some stars changed in brightness over time. She realized that the cycle of brightness could tell her about the size of the star. She could also figure out the distance between stars and Earth. Her discovery made it easier to calculate distances in the universe. Scientists have been able to make other discoveries because of her work.

Margaret Geller (1947-)

Margaret Geller is famous for her work in mapping the universe. Her maps have given us a better understanding of the universe. They also help us to understand how the universe began.

In 1989, Geller helped discover what's known as the **Great Wall**. It's a sheet of galaxies stretching at least 500 million light years. A light year is a unit of distance. It is the distance that light can travel in one year.

Geller was homeschooled as a child. Her father was a chemist. He urged her to study science. Geller was the second woman to earn a Ph.D. in physics from Princeton University. She has also made films about science. These films have won many awards. They have also helped us understand our place in the universe. Geller is still working to uncover the mysteries of the universe.

Did You Know?

One of Geller's most famous discoveries is a stickman figure she saw in the map of the universe. The map contained at least 1,000 galaxies. It extended 500 million light years.

The *Challenger* Disaster

A space shuttle is a spacecraft that can be used over and over to study space beyond Earth's atmosphere. The Space Shuttle *Challenger* flew nine successful missions. On January 28, 1986, *Challenger* lifted off from the Kennedy Space Center. Onboard was a crew of seven. One of the seven was teacher Christa McAuliffe. She was the first member of the Teacher in Space Program.

Seventy-three seconds into the flight, the *Challenger* broke apart. All of the crew were killed. The tragedy was blamed on a faulty seal in the rocket and cold weather. The crew members who died that day are remembered as heroes. They gave their lives for space exploration.

Astronomer: Sandra Faber

University of California Observatories

Telescope Traveler

Imagine looking into space through a powerful telescope. With one look, you could travel billions of miles away—sort of. Sandy Faber "travels" like this all the time.

Faber is an astronomer. She uses powerful telescopes to observe the sky. They let Faber look deep into space and see galaxies forming—all without leaving Earth.

Hubble Telescope

One powerful telescope that Faber uses is the Hubble Space Telescope. Imagine a telescope the size of a school bus. It floats in orbit above our planet. It takes photographs of other planets and stars!

When the Hubble was first put into space, it took blurry pictures. Luckily, Faber is also an expert at designing and fixing telescopes. She told astronauts how to fix the telescope by putting "glasses" on it. It worked!

About You

As a young girl, Faber loved stargazing with her dad. What are your hobbies?

Being There

If you were an astronomer, you would use telescopes, satellites, and other tools. You would explore objects in space. You could also . . .

- investigate planets and moons in our solar system.
- explore the birth of stars.
- search for planets outside our solar system.

4 U 2 Do

What is it like to look into space? You do not need to be an astronomer. You can look at the night sky, too. Use a pair of binoculars, a small telescope, or just your eyes. Can you see the light and dark areas on the moon? Can you locate any planets?

Lab: Collecting Micrometeorites

Did you know that items from outer space can be found in your own backyard? Tiny samples of space rocks float in our atmosphere. They float until dust and water carry them to the ground. These rock samples are micrometeorites. The best time to collect them is after a meteor shower.

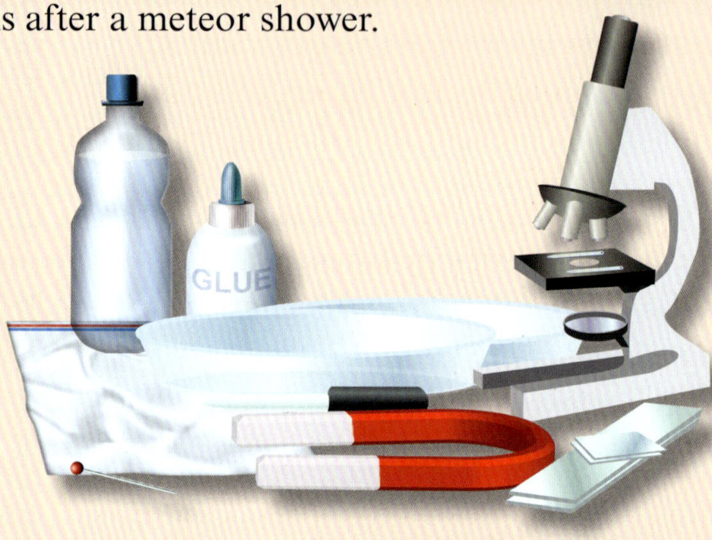

Materials

- 2 shallow dishes (heat resistant)
- distilled water (about 2 cups—enough to fill a dish)
- magnet
- plastic wrap or sandwich bag
- heat source for boiling water (optional)
- microscope or magnifying glass
- 2 microscope slides and covers
- mounting glue
- eyedropper
- sewing needle or large pin

Procedures

1 Place a dish outside to collect rainwater. Or leave the dish outside for a few days.

2 Cover a magnet with plastic wrap or a sandwich bag. Sweep the covered magnet through the water in the collecting dish, especially the bottom and sides. (Micrometeors are rich in iron, so they will stick to the magnet.)

3 Fill a second dish with distilled water. Place the covered magnet in the dish filled with distilled water. Remove the plastic from the magnet and gently swirl it around to allow the micrometeors to fall to the bottom of the dish.

4 Remove the plastic from the distilled water. Boil the water in the dish until it evaporates. (Ask an adult for help.) Or, let it evaporate naturally.

5 Magnetize a needle or pin by rubbing it on the magnet for about a minute. Drag the pin or needle along the sides and bottom of the dish.

6 Tap the needle or pin onto a microscope slide so samples fall onto the slide.

7 Glue down a cover glass. Examine the particles. Any rounded and pitted metallic particles are probably micrometeorites!

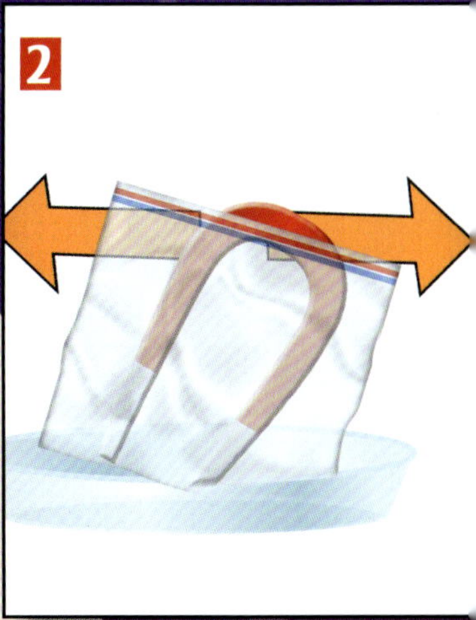

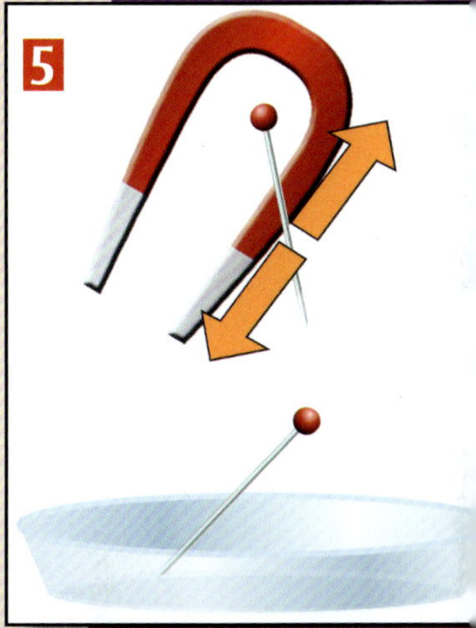

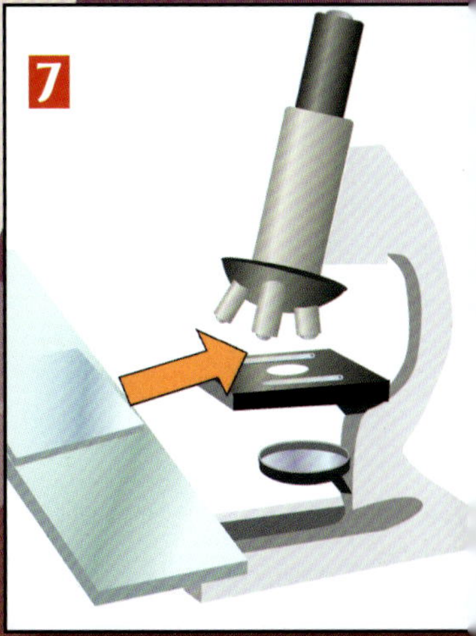

Glossary

astronomer—a person who studies celestial objects

astronomy—the scientific study of the universe and of objects in space, such as the moon, the sun, planets, and stars

constellations—patterns formed by stars

gravity—a force that pulls objects together

Great Wall—Margaret Geller's discovery of a sheet of galaxies stretching at least 500 million light years

heretic—a person who doesn't conform to the established attitudes or beliefs of a church

light year—the distance that light can travel in one year

Milky Way—the spiral galaxy in which our solar system exists

NASA—National Aeronautics and Space Administration

observatory—a building or place designed for making astronomical observations

solar system—one or more stars with orbiting planets

stars—large, luminous points in space that are made of gases

telescope—a device that uses lenses to make distant objects appear closer and larger

Index

Sally Ride Science

Sally Ride Science™ is an innovative content company dedicated to fueling young people's interests in science. Our publications and programs provide opportunities for students and teachers to explore the captivating world of science—from astrobiology to zoology. We bring science to life and show young people that science is creative, collaborative, fascinating, and fun.

Image Credits

Cover: Paul LeFevre/Shutterstock; p.3 NASA; p.4 The Granger Collection, New York; p.5 NASA; p.6 (top) Photos.com; p.6 (bottom) Diego Barucco/Shutterstock; p.7 Public Domain; p.8 Mary Evans Picture Library/Alamy; p.9 (background) Jaimie Duplass/Shutterstock; p.9 Patrick Breig/Shutterstock; p.10 (top) Jurgen Ziewe/Shutterstock; p.10 (left) The Granger Collection, New York; p.10 (bottom) Jurgen Ziewe/Shutterstock; p.11 (background) William Attard McCarthy/Shutterstock; p.11 Jasenka Lukša/Shutterstock; 12 (top) William Attard McCarthy/Shutterstock; p.12 (left) Photos.com; p.12 (bottom) Stephen Girimont/Shutterstock; p.12 (bottom left) SuperStock, Inc./SuperStock; p.13 NASA; p.13 (bottom) Germany Feng/Shutterstock; p.14 SuperStock, Inc./ SuperStock; p.15 Time & Life Pictures/Getty Images; p.16 (top) Photos.com; p.16 (left) Library of Congress; p.16 (bottom) Visual Arts Library (London)/Alamy; p.17 (left) Photos.com; p.17 (right) Harris Shiffman/iStockphoto; p.18 J. Helgason/Shutterstock; p.19 (background) Prisma/SuperStock; p.19 (top) Mary Evans Picture Library/Alamy; p.20 (top) NASA; p.20 (bottom) Science Source/Photo Researchers; p.21 NASA; p.22 Getty Images; p.23 (background) Photos.com; p.23 Harvard College Observatory/Photo Researchers, Inc.; p.24 NASA; p.24 (left) Massimo Ramella; p.24 (bottom) NASA; p.25 Dennis Sabo/Shutterstock; p.25 (right) NASA; p.26 (bottom) NASA MSFC; p.26–27 NASA MSFC; p.27 Paul LeFevre/Shutterstock; p.28 (top) NASA; p.28–29 Nicoll Rager Fuller